SIMPLE MACHINES

WEDGES

ARE MACHINES

T0020342

DOUGLAS BENDER

A Crabtree Roots Plus Book

CRABTREE
Publishing Company
www.crabtreebooks.com

School-to-Home Support for Caregivers and Teachers

This book helps children grow by letting them practice reading. Here are a few guiding questions to help the reader with building his or her comprehension skills. Possible answers appear here in red.

Before Reading:

- What do I think this book is about?
  - *I think this book is about wedges.*
  - *I think this book is about the many ways we use wedges in our everyday lives.*
- What do I want to learn about this topic?
  - *I want to learn how I can use wedges.*
  - *I want to learn why wedges are called simple machines.*

During Reading:

- I wonder why...
  - *I wonder why a doorstop is called a wedge.*
  - *I wonder why a wedge can help us cut things.*
- What have I learned so far?
  - *I have learned learned that wedges can be big or small.*
  - *I have learned that an axe is a wedge.*

After Reading:

- What details did I learn about this topic?
  - *I have learned that my teeth can be wedges.*
  - *I have learned that a pair of scissors has two wedges that cut when they come together.*
- Read the book again and look for the vocabulary words.
  - *I see the word **axe** on page 16 and the word **apple** on page 20. The other vocabulary words are found on page 23.*

This is a **wedge**.

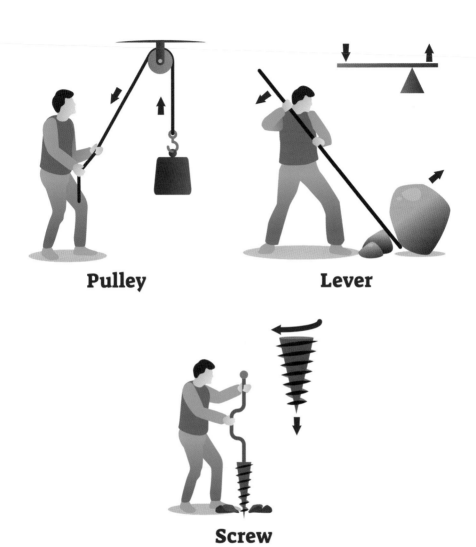

Pulley

Lever

Screw

It is one of six
simple machines.

Wedge

Inclined Plane

Wheel and Axle

Simple machines have few or no moving parts.

Wedges can help hold things in place. Pushpins are wedges.

Wedges can help cut things. Scissors have two wedges. They cut when they come together.

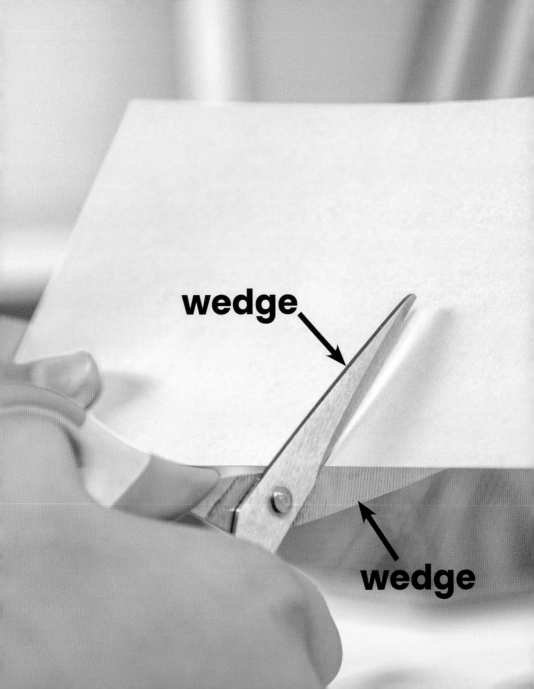

wedge

wedge

This machine has a big wedge. It pushes the dirt.

This zipper has a small wedge. It splits apart the zipper.

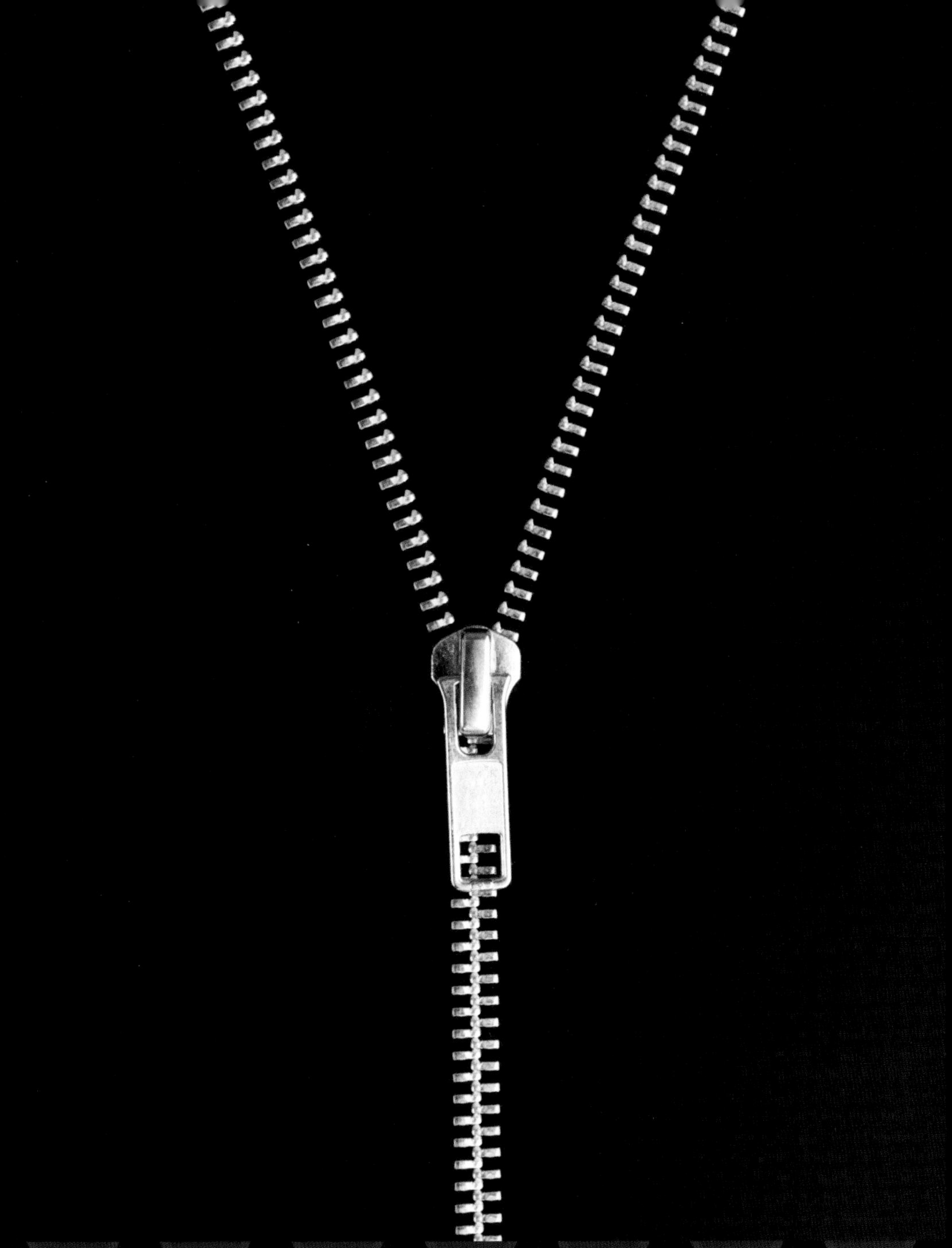

A **doorstop** is a wedge.

It holds the door open.

An **axe** is a wedge.

It can cut wood.

A **tooth** can
be a wedge!

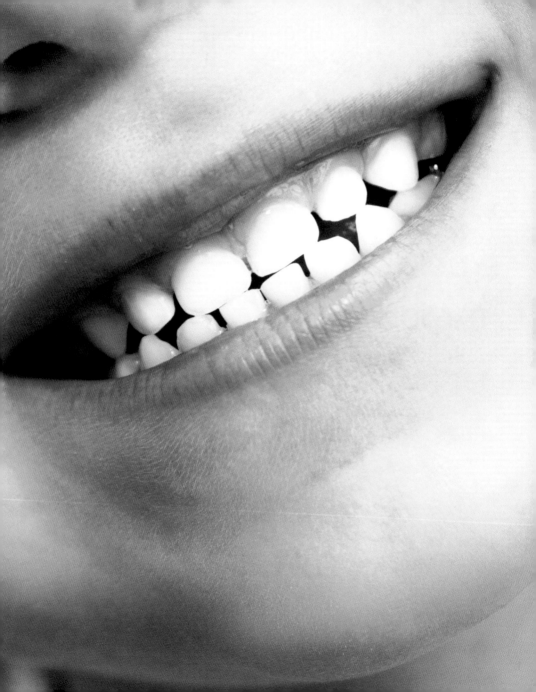

Your teeth cut through food.

Cam takes a bite of an **apple**.

Word List
Sight Words

a	help	parts
an	helps	place
are	hold	small
be	holds	the
big	in	things
can	is	this
cut	it	through
door	moving	to
few	no	wood
food	open	your
have	or	

Words to Know

apple

axe

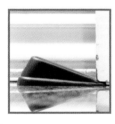

doorstop

Wedge

simple machines

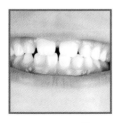

tooth

wedge

CRABTREE
Publishing Company

Written by: Douglas Bender
Designed by: Rhea Wallace
Series Development: James Earley
Proofreader: Janine Deschenes
Production coordinator
 and Prepress technician: Katherine Berti
Print coordinator: Katherine Berti
Educational Consultant: Marie Lemke M.Ed.

Photographs:
Shutterstock: Starodubtsev Kostantin: cover, p.
 1; alicja neumiler: p. 3, 23; Sathitanont N: p. 7;
 Veja: p. 9; Smileus: p. 11; Keisuke: p. 13; Karynf: p.
 14-15, 23; Noerenberg: p. 16, 23; tramper79: p. 17;
 Stobabox: p. 19, 23; Africa Studio: p. 21, 23

SIMPLE MACHINES

WEDGES
ARE MACHINES

Library and Archives Canada
Cataloguing in Publication

CIP available at Library and Archives Canada

Library of Congress
Cataloging-in-Publication Data

CIP available at Library of Congress

Crabtree Publishing Company

www.crabtreebooks.com   1-800-387-7650   Printed in the U.S.A./CG20210915/012022

Published in the United States
Crabtree Publishing
347 Fifth Avenue, Suite 1402-145
New York, NY, 10016

Published in Canada
Crabtree Publishing
616 Welland Ave.
St. Catharines, ON, L2M 5V6